Acknowledgments

To my support system,
you know who you are!

Thank you for your prayers,
laughter and love.

I dedicate this part
of my journey to my father.

I promised you this day would come!

Xoxo, R.J.

Educators and librarians, for a variety of teaching tools, visit us at:

www.adventuresofalleykats.com

ISBN-13: 978-0-692-49119-5

Contents

In the beginning…

DING, DONG

The doorbell rings at the quiet residence located on 1070 Sunnyside Ct, in the small town of Harborville, USA.

"Hey Al, Al! ALBERT! Maybe you should turn the volume down on your headphones. Can you get the door? I think its Leyla."

Kattie Marie Burns, but everyone calls her Kat. She spends most of her time with her good friend Leyla who moved to the neighborhood from California, five years ago. Kat's cousin Albert or Al, lives across town and rides the bus home with Kat everyday because his parents work late hours at the hospital.

You can always find the three children hanging out in Kat's room but they refer to it as the "Alleykats Headquarters," within the headquarters is a secret door for the Alleykats to move safely through their adventures.

Kat's a huge collector of old history books and letters that her grandfather gave her when she was six years old and she's been collecting them ever since. Kat's dream is to be an Archivist when she graduates from college. An Archivist is a person that keeps the history of a building, culture, or thing in a safe place, so they usually have one of kind items.

"I didn't hear you Kat. I was in the middle of mixing a beat; DJ Cool Breeze is so cool. His library of music is crazy good," yells Al. He hesitates for a minute while enjoying the musical beats tap dancing on his eardrums. "Oh yeah, the door," says Al as he jumps out of the chair charging for the door.

"BOO!" screams Leyla as she walks in Kat's room. "Did I scare you?" Kat turns around in her chair and responds, "NEVER!" All three of them chuckle. "Your mom let me in and told me you were in here, what are you doing Kat?" asked Leyla as she plops on the bed with a book. "I'm trying to do my homework, but I'm not understanding the assignment right now. I'm not really good at remembering all of the Presidents," Kat mumbled.

NEW MESSAGE!

"Looks like we have a new message! The adventure begins," shouts Al.

Al, Leyla, and Kat form the super sleuth group named "Alleykats." Albert Clemons is the Hip Hop Librarian that loves all things music and always keeps his trademark headphones with him. Al's favorite music is from the 70s and 80s. His love for music comes from his Creole roots thanks to his maternal grandmother who still lives in New Orleans, Louisiana and his love of Hip Hop derives from his dad, who's from the neighborhood of Harlem in New York City.

Leyla Harris on the other hand is the sleuth that pieces the story together. Leyla spent the first six years of her life in California and then her family moved to the small town of Harborville, USA. Leyla often refers to herself as the "melting pot" coming from a multicultural background. She calls herself the Oral Historian, because she's very accurate with her storytelling. Where might Leyla get her information from to tell the stories? Kat, that's who, since she is the Archivist and Al has the gift of creating a catalog of everything they do.

"It says something about a missing link." Kat continues to read, "With this person we would not be united." Kat looks puzzled while

looking at the computer screen and adjusting her glasses on her face. "I've got it!" Al shouts with excitement, "It must be Martin Luther King Jr. We know where he is, mystery solved. He united the people, no missing link there." Kat and Leyla give Al the piercing look of disgust and confusion. "Well, this time you are wrong my music loving cousin, because there is a riddle," says Kat. Al frowns as he maneuvers his headphones around his large mane of hair to listen closely.

"Birth place was in Kentucky, then I made my way to Mississippi, then on to Presidency."

"So we are going to Kentucky or Mississippi?" Al asked. "We must always start at the beginning, so the clue says Kentucky," responds Leyla with her puzzle piece clutched in her hand.

Each Alleykat carries a symbol of their secret gift in their hand whenever it's time to set out on an adventure. Al carries a sheet of paper that's rolled very neatly as if it should go in time capsule or bottle. Leyla carries a puzzle piece to help connect the dots during travel for solving the mysteries and Kat carries a magnifying glass for super sleuth powers when looking for extra clues. Having all three of the pieces along with the help from others throughout the adventure is the only way they are able to move easily through the alley missions.

   "We should be back by dinner this time Al," Kat says, as she opens the "secret" door for the alley. Al replies, "I sure hope so, this time I'm packing a snack." Al runs to get a few snacks to share with the others and gingerly closes the door behind him.

Hello Kentucky, No Derby!

The Alleykats arrive on the other side of the secret alley door and see a sign. Kat screams with excitement, "look it says the State Archives is that way." Al points at the *Welcome to Kentucky* sign. "I must take a picture, you know I love taking pictures whenever we enter a new state," said Leyla.

Al fiddles with his headphones because the Alleykats know they will have to walk many blocks in order to reach the state archives for more answers. Leyla whispers, "Al, I'm glad you packed snacks, we are going to need them! I feel we may be gone awhile."

The Alleykats begin their walk to the State Archives located in Frankfort, Kentucky.

When the Alleykats finally arrive at the state archives, they are greeted by a tall, slim man with green eyes wearing square frame glasses, a short sleeve, plaid, green and yellow button down shirt, and khakis pants. The gentleman is wearing a distinguished pin. Kat recognizes a CAA pin near the collar of his shirt and she knew right away he would have all the answers.

The Alleykats walk up to the man with Kat leading the way. Kat adjusts her glasses and says, "Hi, we are looking for any information of United States Presidents, I noticed your CAA pin and I knew you were the person to ask."

The gentleman clears his throat, "Well, hello

my name is Chris Porter, and you young lady must love the archives, are you a junior member of the Club for American Archivists?" Kat responded with pride, "Well yes...yes I am, and these are my friends, Al and Leyla, we just want to know more about the Presidents that would have a connection with the state of Kentucky." Mr. Porter places his right hand on his face as if he's thinking about what he should do next. He walks over to a middle shelf and pulls a box down that is filled with folders. "The 16th President of the United States was born in Kentucky, and I can get more information on the man they called Honest Abe," says Mr. Porter.

Leyla politely raises her hand, "Excuse me, Mr. Porter, we know about Abraham Lincoln, could there be anyone else? Any other U.S. Presidents?" Mr. Porter replies, "Leyla, did you know we weren't always identified as the United States of America? We were once divided between the north and south." Al's eyes became filled with interest. "That's right, where would we find

10

more information? It may help us to find the person we are looking for," Kat said.

FIRE ALARM SOUNDS

A security guard runs in and yells that everyone must evacuate the building. Leyla screams, "Oh no!" Al grabs the girls' hands and bolts to the nearest exit. Kat pauses and lets out a screech of panic, "but Mr. Porter we aren't finished." Mr. Porter now running in the opposite direction looks back and yells, "Go to Mississippi, a family, last name is Da...a...a..." The door slams as if it were sealed shut behind Mr. Porter and the Alleykats are now standing outside now at the rear of the building after the fire alarm. Leyla says to Kat, "it's okay, we will figure it out." Al begins singing, "M-I-crooked letter-crooked letter-I." The Alleykats enter the alley with a walk of promise as they prepare themselves for the next stop.

M-I-CROOKED LETTER...

"We have arrived!" exclaimed Leyla. Al turns to Leyla and Kat with a grin and says, "The state of Mississippi always reminds me of someone. Can you guess who?" The girls ignore Al, giving him a smirk with impatience written all over their faces and decide to remain focused on the goal. The Alleykats must stay on task or they will run out of time.

"I hope this trip will be quick and no fire/ tornado drills, we have enough of those in school." Leyla jokes with a giggle. The Alleykats enter the State Archives located in the capital city of Jackson, Mississippi. They look around but it seems to be pretty quiet. The Alleykats split up to look down every row to see if there is someone to help them.

Kat becomes rather anxious that she begins to go from a slow paced walk to a power walk. Without looking Kat runs into an elderly woman, standing about five feet, six inches tall with dark brown curly hair wearing a pair of purple oval frame reading glasses. The woman peers over her spectacles with her sparkling light brown eyes and says to Kat, "Are you in a rush my dear?" Kat stood in front of the woman with a stunned look on her face. However, the woman looked very familiar to Kat, but she was too shocked to say anything.

Leyla and Al run over and introduce themselves. "Hello ma'am, my name is Al, and these are my friends Kat and Leyla, and we have some questions for you. Can you please help us?" Al extends his right hand to shake hers. "Well, aren't you a little gentleman, my name is Dorothy Williams but everyone around here calls me Ms. Dollie. It's a pleasure to me you all. Have a seat my little scholars."

Ms. Dollie points to the table with four chairs so they can sit down and chat. Before sitting down Kat apologizes for running into Ms. Dollie. "I am very sorry," Kat whispered. "Oh sweetie, it's okay what do you all need help with," Ms. Dollie says with a warming smile.

"We wanted to know about a President that may have lived in Mississippi," Leyla said. "The only part we understood was a family with the last name that began with D-A when we talked to Mr. Porter in Kentucky. He told us to come here," Al said. The girls give Al the look, you know the look, he's said too much and at risk of getting in trouble.

Ms. Dollie looks puzzled, but begins to share

with the Alleykats what she knows. "You must have talked to Mr. Porter over the phone, she chuckles, well Mr. Ben Montgomery, is a distant relative on my maternal grandmother's side of the family. Mr. Montgomery once lived on Brierfield Plantation, but now you're able to visit a place called Beauvoir. So, I know about the place because I've visited the plantation for help with my family history. So, I know the former owners family history is there. I'm sure the Davis family is who you're looking for."

Al jumps out of the chair and says, "Davis! Brierfield Plantation?" Ms. Dollie explains that two brothers once owned Brierfield Planation. The two brothers were Joseph and Jefferson Davis, but one of the brothers entered politics and had to move to Richmond, Virginia.

Ms. Dollie gave the Alleykats almost the same information that Mr. Porter from Kentucky shared with them. The United States was divided into the North and the South, the north being the Union and the south being the Confederacy.

"So are you saying there were two Presidents?" asked Leyla. Ms. Dollie responds with, "you are correct."

Kat then asked during what time were we divided. "The Civil War, so for sure between 1861 and 1865," said Ms. Dollie. "Where was the capital of the Confederacy? Was it Washington DC like the current President?" inquired Leyla. Ms. Dollie explains that there were in fact a few capitals before the current capital in Richmond, Virginia.

Al suddenly takes off running. Leyla chases after him. "I'm sorry Ms. Dollie, we have to go,"

explains Kat. "Okay be careful," shouts Ms. Dollie, as she waves goodbye to the Alleykats. The Alleykats disappear into the secret alley entrance and blast off to their next location.

Next Stop...The Confederacy

The secret door opens and the Alleykats exit to Richmond, Virginia, home of the Confederacy.

The first building they see is a huge white house ahead. The Alleykats begin sprinting at full speed once they noticed the front door. The white house was massive in size but quite different from the white house they daydreamed about. "Hopefully someone is home to talk to us," said Leyla as she tries to catch her breath. The Alleykats approach the front door but to their surprise the two doors were ajar. "Good day soldiers," states the gentleman in the doorway. "Come on in, wipe your feet, house rule is no outside dirt on the inside." A slender man with an almond brown complexion stood in the doorway adjusting his reading glasses on his nose while flashing a comforting smile inviting the Alleykats inside.

The Alleykats enter the foyer area; the entrance was grand due to the double statues

that greet you upon entering. "Don't mind them, that's Triumph and Laughter, those statues are older than all of us combined. My name is Sergeant Major Allen Hamilton but you all can just call me Sgt. Major."

Sgt. Major extends his right hand to shake their hands and when he gets to Al, "U.S. Army," Al blurts out. "Right you are, soldier!" said Sgt. Major. Kat decides to introduce everyone, "I'm Kattie but I go by Kat, and this is Leyla and that's Al, and we are looking for the President of the Confederacy." Sgt. Major's face lights up and says, "Oh yes, you have come to the right place, follow me into the study room and we can discuss more." The Alleykats file behind Sgt. Major as if they were true marching soldiers.

They were following very closely seeing as though the mansion was larger than life and filled with many entryways. It appeared to be very easy to get lost if you don't know your way around. "Have a seat on the rug," instructs Sgt. Major, "I'll answer any questions you have."

Leyla leads with the first question, "What exactly is a Confederacy?" Sgt. Major begins showing the Alleykats old photos as he begins explaining the importance of the Confederacy.

During the Civil War, the present day United States was divided into two parts, The Union (north) and the Confederacy (south) and the Civil War was also known as the War Between the States. During the war (1861-1865), President Abraham Lincoln was the President of the Union and Jefferson Davis was the President of the Confederacy.

Sgt. Major continues to share stories about the history of the area and takes the Alleykats on a quick tour of the house. Al raised his hand in the middle of the tour with a weird look on his face, "So, Abraham Lincoln and Jefferson Davis were born in Kentucky, but I just think it's odd that I've never heard of Jefferson Davis."

Sgt. Major began telling the Alleykats about the importance of knowing both sides of the story and how history is often written

from a singular point of view. President Davis was responsible for the clean drinking water in Washington DC, designed the statue on the state capitol, a key leader behind establishing the Smithsonian Museum, and the only President of the Confederacy.

The Alleykats have wrapped up the mini tour with Sgt Major. "Wow! I love the Smithsonian; I'm going to add all this information to the History book that the Alleykats are putting together. I mean I can complete my book report about the American Civil War," murmured Kat.

The Alleykats have definitely had a full day and it looks like they will make it home in enough time for dinner with their families. "I'm going to share this information with my family at the dinner table this evening," said Leyla. Kat turns to Sgt. Major and says, "You have been great Sgt. Major, thank you for everything especially the tour, we learned so much." Sgt. Major walks the Alleykats to the door so they can exit the same way they entered. He waves to them from the steps of the white house as the Alleykats walk away.

Leyla turns to Al and Kat to inform them that the next stop is Alleykats Headquarters. "Hey Al," said Leyla, "please tell me you have more snacks...I'm hungry." Al gulps with shame, "No, I ate the last fruit snack when you both were in the bathroom." The girls laugh as they enter the alley feeling accomplished.

Headquarters Wrap-up

"What a day, what an amazing day, what an eventful day," says Leyla as she exits the alley back into the headquarters. Kat looks at the wall clock, and notices that it's almost time for dinner. "Hey Al, are you staying for dinner tonight," Kat inquires. "Leyla has to be home in thirty minutes. I was going to walk her half way home." Al walks to the corner to grab his backpack, "No my mom doesn't work late tonight. She's picking me up; I hope she cooks some of my favorites. I'm so hungry now."

DING, DONG

The Alleykats walk towards the front door after hearing the doorbell. Al's mom was on the other side of the doorway greeting them with the biggest smile. She was early picking Al up. Al hugs his mom and asks if Leyla could receive a ride home from Kat's house. Al's mom said,

"Absolutely, I have no problem taking Leyla home, and Al, I purchased your favorite chicken to enjoy for dinner." Al's face beams with joy. "Kentucky's Favorite Chicken! SWEET! I would rather call it my favorite chicken mom, I have had enough of Kentucky for the day," Al said jokingly. Leyla and Kat giggle as Leyla and Al exit the front door of Kat's house. Kat closes the door, and runs to the kitchen to help set the table for dinner.

Kat couldn't wait to tell her family about the President that was once missing from the history books, but thanks to the Alleykats, the story is now complete.

CASE CLOSED!

To learn more about the Civil War Museum,
White House of the Confederacy,
and the family of President Jefferson Davis
please visit:

American Civil War Museum
(formerly Museum of the Confederacy)
1201 E. Clay Street
Richmond, VA 23219
www.acwm.org

www.ingramcontent.com/pod-product-compliance
Lightning Source LLC
Chambersburg PA
CBHW041804040426
42448CB00001B/37